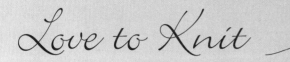

Love to Knit

KNITTING FOR GOLD

Dedication

I would like to dedicate this book to my Mother, to my children
Shaun and Jenny, to the Materialistics knitting group that meet
at the Customs House in South Shields, and to all the women of
the Washington Bridge Women's Support and Education Centre,
where I volunteer.

Love to Knit

KNITTING FOR GOLD

Sue McBride

Search Press

Acknowledgements

I would like to thank a couple of people who have really
helped me with this book: my daughter Jenny, who
organises me and is a whizz with the computer;
Brenda Royal, who did some test knitting for me to see
if the dolls would actually work; and E. Kemps,
of Chester Road, Sunderland, the shop where I get
all my supplies.

First published in Great Britain 2012

Search Press Limited
Wellwood, North Farm Road,
Tunbridge Wells, Kent TN2 3DR

Text copyright © Sue McBride 2012

Photographs by Paul Bricknell at Search Press Photographic Studio

Photographs and design copyright © Search Press Ltd. 2012

ISBN: 978-1-84448-791-2

The Publishers and author can accept no responsibility for any
consequences arising from the information, advice or instructions given
in this publication.

Suppliers
If you have difficulty in obtaining any of the materials and equipment
mentioned in this book, then please visit the Search Press website for
details of suppliers: www.searchpress.com

Printed in China

Contents

Introduction

Small toys are among my favourite things to knit. They are fantastic to give away as gifts or to send to charity fairs for a good cause. I have been knitting for almost fifty years so I have made a few!

This book is packed full of patterns to make twenty sporting figures. Ten male and ten female athletes, all with their own outfits and the equipment needed for their particular sport, are waiting for you to knit them into action.

With changes of yarn colour for skin and hair, your athlete can come from anywhere in the world that you can imagine. You can give them character and personality by changing their facial features and hairstyles. I have to admit that one or two bear a very close resemblance to several people that I know.

The clothes are designed to be removed, so you can have one athlete with as many outfits as you like, or you can make several figures and dress them in your favourite team or country's colours to hold your own track meet, soccer match or even a downhill ski event.

These patterns are designed to be suitable for all levels of knitting ability. If you are starting out, try knitting the runner (see page 14), and if you fancy more of a challenge, try those with a little more detail such as the ice hockey player (see page 58) or archer (see page 48). There is something for everyone, even for knitters who try to avoid sewing up, as there is a tennis dress which has no seams and requires only minimal sewing.

You can keep your sports star for yourself as a mascot, or give them away to your friends – they take no time at all to make. The dolls were fun to dream up, and I am sure everyone who receives one will love them. Most of all I hope you have a lot of fun with this book.

Get ready

Materials

Each of the projects in this book includes a list of the materials and equipment that you will need to make that particular sports doll, and his or her equipment and kit.

Yarn

All of the quantities of yarn given in the book are to be regarded as approximate. Some of the projects in this book include unusual yarns such as variegated ribbon yarn, but unless noted otherwise, all of the yarns used are Double Knitting weight, abbreviated to DK. DK yarns are also known as 8-ply or worsted.

Needles

I have used the same size needles for all of the projects in this book: 3mm, which is equivalent to UK size 11, and US size 3. I always use straight steel needles, but the type does not really matter: the patterns will still work if you prefer to use other needles, such as bamboo.

Tension

The tension used throughout for the DK yarn is 26 sts and 32 rows to a 10cm (4in) square. The ribbon yarn used for the swimming costume (see page 52) and the doubled metallic yarn used for the rhythmic gymnast's leotard (see page 32) and the ice skater's dress (see page 42) are also worked at the same tension.

The tension for the 4-ply yarn used in the archer's outfit (see pages 48–51) is 28 sts and 36 rows to a 10cm (4in) square.

If you are getting more sts and rows than this you are knitting too tightly and so need to use a larger needle. If your work is turning out to be larger, then use a smaller needle.

Stuffing

The appearance of the figures can be changed greatly by the way they are stuffed. They have all been knitted with the same basic male or female pattern (see pages 10–11), but in real life a runner would not have the same physique as a weightlifter. Stuff the figure lightly to give a slim appearance, suitable for gymnastics or long-distance running, and pad out others, such as the weightlifter, to give the appearance of rippling muscles and bulging biceps.

Raglan seams

Some of the projects include raglan seams for sleeves. A raglan seam is where the slanted decreased edge of the sleeve is stitched to the front or back decreased armhole edge. Because of this slant there is a lot of stretch, so it is best to pin it in place, matching the cast-off stitches of the underarm to the sleeve.

With the wrong sides of the work together, pin the left-hand edge of the front to the left edge of the sleeve. Pin the right edge of the front to the right edge of another sleeve, then sew together with mattress stitch, so you can see where your stitches are going in order to produce a flatter seam. Work the back raglan seams in the same way.

Sewing up

I mainly use mattress stitch for sewing up as it gives a flatter seam. If the yarn you have used for the body is cotton, split it and use two strands of the yarn. If it is not strong enough use two strands of sewing thread in a colour that matches your yarn.

ABBREVIATIONS

sts	stitches
K	knit
P	purl
K2tog	knit two together
P2tog	purl two together
M1	make one
sl1	slip one
psso	pass slip stitch over
skpo	slip a stitch, knit the next stitch, then pass the slipped stitch over the knit one
inc	increase
dec	decrease
rem	remaining
rep	repeat
yo	yarn over
tbl	through the back of the loop
GS	garter stitch (consecutive rows of knit stitch only)
SS	stocking stitch (alternating rows of knit and purl). Unless instructed otherwise, always start with a knit row.

Basic dolls

You will need

Needles 3mm (US 3)

Yarns 50g balls of DK yarn in skin colour and hair colour of your choice
Small amount of DK yarn in underwear colour of your choice

Sewing needle and thread in skin colour of your choice

Toy stuffing

Male figure

Feet

Make two.
Cast on 5sts in the skin colour.
rows 1–2: SS.
row 3: K1, M1, K3, M1, K1.
row 4: purl.
row 5: K1, M1, K5, M1, K1.
rows 6–14: SS.
row 15: skpo, K5, K2tog.
row 16: purl.
row 17: K1, M1, K5, M1, K1.
rows 18–26: SS.
row 27: skpo, K5, K2tog.
row 28: purl.
row 29: skpo, K3, K2tog.
row 30: purl.
Cast off.

Head

Cast on 10 sts in the skin colour.
row 1: purl.
row 2: inc in every st.
row 3: purl.
row 4: (K1, inc1) to end.
rows 5–21: SS beg with P row.
row 22: (K1, K2tog) to end.
row 23: purl.
row 24: K2tog to end.
Break yarn and thread through all sts.

Arms

Make two.
Cast on 4sts in the skin colour.
row 1: purl.
rows 2: inc 1 st in first and last st.
rows 3–10: rep rows 1 and 2 four times.
rows 11–37: SS beg with P row.
row 38: K2tog to end.
Break yarn and thread through sts.

Legs and torso

Cast on 14sts in the skin colour.
rows 1–20: SS.
row 21: K1, M1, K12, M1, K1.
rows 22–26: SS.
row 27: K1, M1, K14, M1, K1.
rows 28–32: SS.
Break yarn and put sts on a holder, then make a second leg in the same way. Join in white yarn for underpants.
rows 33–42: SS, knitting across both legs.
Break off yarn and join in skin colour.
rows 43–52: SS.
row 53: K7, skpo, K2tog, K14, skpo, K2tog, K7.
row 54: purl.
row 55: K6, skpo, K2tog, K12, skpo, K2tog, K6.
row 56: purl.
row 57: K5, skpo, K2tog, K10, skpo, K2tog, K5.
row 58: purl.
row 59: K2tog to end.
rows 60–61: rep rows 58 and 59.
Break yarn and thread through all sts.

Hair base

Cast on 40 sts in the hair colour.
rows 1–6: GS.
row 7: (K6, K2tog) to end.
row 8: knit.
row 9: (K5, K2tog) to end.
row 10: knit.
row 11: (K4, K2tog) to end.
row 12: knit.
row 13: (K3, K2tog) to end.
row 14: knit.
row 15: (K2, K2tog) to end.
row 16: knit.
row 17: (K1, K2tog) to end.
row 18: knit.
row 19: K2tog to end.
Break yarn and thread through remaining sts.
Sew up row ends. With seam at the back, stitch to head.

Making up

1 Fold the feet in half so that the cast-on and cast-off edges meet. Use a needle and thread to sew the sides together. Stuff lightly, then sew the cast on and cast off edges together.

2 Sew up each leg seam to the crotch. Sew the back seam to halfway up. Stuff the legs and lower body. Stitch further up the back seam, stuffing as you go. Open up the neck where the stitches are gathered and stuff to the top then pull the neck hole shut and sew down the back in the remaining yarn.

3 Pull the yarn tight where it is threaded through the last worked row of the head. Stitch the row ends together for the back seam. Stuff the head firmly but do not overstuff, as it will be too big to get the clothes on. Place on top of the neck with the seam at the back and sew the head to the body.

4 Pull up the the yarn threaded through the last row of stitches of the arm and sew the arm seam. Stuff up to the seam top. Sew the arms to the body, one on each side, starting with the cast on edge just below the head seam, stitching the armhole in an oval shape. Put a little stuffing into the top of the arm space just before closing the seam.

5 Starting ten rows up from the end of the arm, run a thread in flesh-coloured yarn all the way round the end of the arm, securing at the seam and finishing where you started. Draw the yarn up a little to define the wrist, then fasten off.

6 Sew a foot to the bottom of each leg, starting with the back of the leg at the back of the foot and stitching the leg on to the top of the foot.

7 Sew the hair on to the head, placing the edge of the back seam at the back of the neck. Backstitch all the way round with the same colour yarn as the hair.

8 Embroider the face using a few small stitches and small lengths of yarn.

Female figure

Work two feet, one head, two arms as male figure. Work legs and torso as male figure to row 26.

rows 27–32: SS across both legs.
row 33: K6, skpo, K2tog, K12, skpo, K2tog, K6.
row 34: purl
row 35: K5, skpo, K2tog, K10, skpo, K2tog, K5.
rows 36–42: SS.
Inc for bust as follows:
row 43: K8, (M1, inc1) three times, K2, (inc1, M1) three times, K8.
rows 44–46: SS.
row 47: K7, skpo, K2tog (sl1, K2tog, psso) twice, K2, (sl1, K2tog, psso) twice, skpo, K2tog, K7.
row 48: purl.
row 49: K6, skpo, K2tog, K4, skpo, K2tog, K6.
rows 50–51: rep rows 48–49.

Make up as for male figure. To give the bust more definition, work a running stitch in the same yarn in a circle on each side of her chest just above the decrease stitches and just below the increase stitches. Pull up and fasten off, then stuff from the back.

The underwear detailed below is used for some of the female projects, but not all.

Knickers

Cast on 18 sts in the underwear colour.
rows 1–2: SS.
rows 3–10: dec each end of every row.
rows 11–16: SS on the 2 sts left.
rows 17–24: inc at both ends of every row.
rows 25–26: SS. Cast off.

Sports bra

Cast on 34 sts in the underwear colour.
rows 1–2: SS.
row 3: K10, cast off 14, K to end. Put the first 10 sts on a holder.
row 4: work on last 10 sts, P.
row 5: skpo, K to last 2 sts, K2tog.
rows 6–11: rep rows 4 and 5 three times.
rows 12–27: GS. Cast off.
Put first 10 sts back on the needle and work from row 4 to match.

Making up

1 Sew up the front of the bra for 1cm (½in).
2 Sew the shoulder straps to the back of the cast-off edge.
3 Sew up the side seams of the knickers.

The completed male and female dolls, ready to be kitted out for their training and competition. The hair on the male doll has been knitted with fun fur to give a fluffy appearance, while the female doll has long strands of yarn stitched on for longer hair (see page 48 for the instructions for this particular hairstyle).

The female doll, modelling the underwear.

The front and back of the underwear.

In Training

You will need

Needles 3mm (US 3)

Yarns 100g balls of DK yarn in pink, blue, white and grey
Small amount of DK yarn in light brown
Sewing needle and thread
Toy stuffing

Athlete

1 Make a male figure in pink with white underpants, and hair base in light brown.
2 Cut some 10cm (4in) strands of light brown yarn and lay them across the hair piece. Using back stitch, sew along the middle to make a parting from the front to the back of the head.
3 Stitch smaller pieces of yarn to the front cast-on edge of the hair piece, and cut the hair to style it.

Trousers

Make two. Cast on 25 sts in blue.
row 1: K1, (P1, K1) to end.
row 2: P1, (K1, P1) to end.
rows 3–28: SS.
rows 29–30: cast off 2 sts at beg of each row.
row 31: skpo, K to last 2 sts, K2tog.
rows 32–38: SS.
rows 39–40: rep rows 1 and 2. Cast off in rib.

Making up

1 Fold each leg in half, then sew up the seam to the point where 2 sts were cast off.
2 Sew the two leg pieces together.

Hooded top

Back

Cast on 23 sts in blue.
rows 1–2: as rows 1 and 2 of trousers.
rows 3–18: SS.
rows 19–20: cast off 3 sts at beg of each row.
row 21: skpo, K to last 2 sts, K2tog.
row 22: purl.
rows 23–28: rep rows 21 and 22 three times. Cast off.

Front

Cast on 23 sts in blue.
rows 1–2: as rows 1 and 2 of trousers.
row 3: K17, turn, P11, put the 6 sts left at each side on holders.

rows 4–7: working on centre 11 sts only, SS.
row 8: skpo, K7, K2tog.
rows 9–12: SS. Break yarn and put these sts on a holder.
With right side of work facing and using left side sts, put sts on a needle and cast on 11 sts. K across cast on sts and 6 sts that were on holder.
Purl across sts just worked and the 6 sts from other side that were left on holder.
next 8 rows: SS.
next row: K7, hold needle with pocket sts in front of needle with main piece sts on, and knit a stitch from each needle together until all pocket sts have been used. K to end of row.
next 7 rows: SS. Work as back from row 19.

Sleeves

Make two. Cast on 19 sts in blue.
rows 1–2: as rows 1 and 2 of back.
rows 3–12: SS.
row 14: inc 1 st at each end of row.
rows 15–20: SS.
rows 21–22: cast off 2 sts at beg of each row.
row 23: skpo, K to last 2 sts, K2tog.
row 24: purl.
rows 25–30: rep rows 23 and 24 three times. Cast off.

Hood

Cast on 21 sts in blue.
row 1: purl.
row 2: inc in every st.
rows 3–22: SS.
row 23: K19, skpo, K2tog, K19.
row 24: purl.
row 25: K18, skpo, K2tog, K18.
row 26: purl.
row 27: K17, skpo, K2tog, K17.
row 28: purl.
row 29: K16, skpo, K2tog, K16.
row 30: purl.
row 31: k15, skpo, P2tog, k15.
row 32: purl. Cast off.

Making up

1 Fold the hood in half so the row ends meet. The cast-off edge will be at the top, folded in half. Sew this seam up, starting at the front.
2 Sew raglan shoulder seams (see page 8). Sew up the side and sleeve seams.
3 Pick up and knit 34sts around the front of the hood. Cast off purlwise.
4 Sew the hood to the neck edge, starting at the middle of the front so that the edges meet. Do not stitch too tightly or the head will not go through the neck of the hooded top.

Trainers

Sole

Make two. Cast on 6 sts in grey.
rows 1–2: SS.
row 3: inc each end of row.
rows 4–10: SS beg with P row.
row 11: skpo, K to last 2 sts, K2tog.
row 12: purl.
rows 13–14: rep rows 11 and 12. Cast off.

Upper

Make two. Cast on 26 sts in white.
row 1: K11, skpo, K2tog, K11.
row 2: purl.
row 3: K10, skpo, K2tog, K10.
row 4: purl.
row 5: K9, skpo, K2tog, K9.
row 6: purl. Cast off.

Making up

1 Sew up the back seam of the upper.
2 Pin the sole to the cast-on edge of the upper, then stitch the upper all the way round the sole.
3 Make laces by oversewing through the cast off sts of the upper. Repeat for the other shoe.

Carl Starsky is an all-round athlete. Dedication is what you need to succeed in athletics and sports events, so he regards a tracksuit and trainers that let him train in all weathers as vital equipment.

Running

Athlete

1 Make a male figure in brown with white underpants, and hair base in black.
2 Stitch short black stitches all over the hair base.

Shorts

Make two. Cast on 26 sts in light blue.
rows 1–6: SS.
rows 7–8: cast off 2 sts at beg of each row.
row 9: skpo, K to last 2 sts, K2tog.
rows 10–20: beg with a P row, SS.
Cast off.

Making up

1 Fold the leg piece in half and sew the row ends together.
2 Sew the leg pieces together from the cast-off sts to the waist.

Top

Back

Cast on 22 sts in yellow.
rows 1–14: SS.
rows 15–16: cast off 2 sts at beg of each row.
row 17: skpo, K to last 2 sts, K2tog.
row 18: purl.
rows 19–22: rep rows 17 and 18 twice more.
rows 23–26: SS.
Cast off.

Front

Follow the instructions for the back to row 22.
row 23: K3, cast off 6 sts, K2.
rows 24–30: work on the last 3 sts for shoulder strap. Cast off
rows 20–26: rejoin yarn to 3 sts left, beg with a P row, work to match first shoulder strap.

Making up

1 Sew up the side seams.
2 Stitch the shoulder straps to the cast-off edge of the back.

Trainers

Make two, following the instructions on page 12. Use yellow for the uppers, grey for the soles and blue for the laces.

You will need

Needles 3mm (US 3)

Yarns 50g balls of DK yarn in brown, light blue and yellow
Small amounts of DK yarn in black, grey and white

Sewing needle and thread
Toy stuffing

Tito Rodriguez storms over the finishing line and throws his hands to the air –his kit is very simple, so there will be plenty of time for celebration.

Football

Athlete

Make a male figure in light brown with white underpants, and hair in brown.

Shorts

Make a pair of shorts following the instructions for shorts on page 14, using red yarn.

Football boots

Make two, following the instructions for trainers on page 12. Use black for the uppers, soles and laces.

Next, stitch four small stitches on top of each other using black yarn in two parallel lines down the sole of the shoe to represent studs.

Shirt

Back

Cast on 22 sts in red.

row 1: knit.

rows 2–15: change to white, then work SS, beg with a K row.

rows 16–17: cast off 2 sts at beg of each row.

row 18: skpo, K to last 2 sts, K2tog.

row 19: purl.

rows 20–27: SS. Cast off.

Front

Follow the instructions for the back to row 17.

row 18: skpo, K5, K2tog, turn.

row 19: purl.

row 20: K5, K2tog.

row 21: purl.

row 22: K4, K2tog.

row 23: purl.

row 24: K3, K2tog.

row 25: purl.

row 26: K2, K2tog.

row 27: purl. Cast off.

Rejoin yarn to sts left and work as from row 18 to match other side of front.

Sleeves

Make two. Cast on 20 sts in red.

row 1: knit.

rows 2–7: change to white, work SS, beg with a K row.

rows 8–9: cast off 2 sts at beg of next 2 rows.

row 10: skpo, K to last 2 sts, K2tog.

row 11: purl.

rows 12–17: rep rows 10 and 11 three times. Cast off.

Making up

1 Sew up the left shoulder seam of the front piece.

2 With red yarn, pick up and knit 8 sts from the back of the neck, 10 sts down the left front, and 10 sts up the right front.

3 Cast off knitwise.

4 Sew up the right shoulder seam.

5 Sew the top of each sleeve into an armhole.

6 Sew up the side and sleeve seams.

Football

Cast on 5 sts in white.

row 1: purl.

row 2: inc in every st.

row 3: purl.

row 4: (K1, inc1) to end.

row 5: purl.

row 6: (K2, inc1) to end.

rows 7–15: SS.

row 16: (K2, K2tog) to end.

row 17: purl.

row 18: (K1, K2tog) to end.

row 19: purl.

row 20: K2tog to end.

Making up

1 Break yarn and thread through sts.

2 Sew up the seam, leaving enough space to stuff the ball firmly. Close seam.

Little Pepé is a flamboyant soccer player, who likes nothing better than showing off his skills to his adoring fans. Next year he might even try to score some goals!

Tennis

Athlete

1 Make a female figure in pink, and hair base in doubled 4-ply tan yarn.

2 Fold some 30cm (11¾in) strands of 4-ply tan yarn in half, thread the looped ends through the cast-on edge of the hair, pull the cut ends through the loop and knot at the front.

3 Take six strands and make tight plaits from the cast-on edge. Tie all the plaits together with yarn at the nape of the neck. Divide the plaits into three groups and make a larger plait with them. Tie the yarn round the bottom of this plait, then trim the long ends off.

Shoes

Make two, following the instructions on page 12. Use white for the uppers, soles and laces.

Dress

Cast on 70 sts in aqua.

rows 1–14: change to white. SS.

row 15: (K5, K2tog) to end.

rows 16–18: SS.

row 19: cast on 20 sts purlwise for tie.

row 20: cast off 42 sts purlwise, P to end.

row 21: cast on 20 sts, cast off 20 sts, K18 (19 sts on needle) yo, K2tog, K14, yo, K2tog, K1.

rows 22–27: SS, beg with P row.

row 28: cast off 2 sts, P until 17 sts rem, turn.

row 29: cast off 2 sts, K to end.

row 30: purl.

row 31: skpo, K to last 2 sts, K2tog.

rows 32–33: rep rows 30 and 31 once more.

row 34: purl. Break off white. Change to aqua.

row 35: knit.

Cast off knitwise with aqua. Put remaining sts on a needle and rejoin white yarn.

next 2 rows: with wrong side facing, cast off 2 sts at beg of each row.

next row: purl.

next row: skpo, K to last 2 sts, K2tog.

next 2 rows: rep last two rows once more.

next row: change to aqua. K. Cast off knitwise.

Armhole edging and making up

1 With right side facing, pick up and knit 16 sts evenly along armhole edge.

2 Cast on 8 sts purlwise for shoulder strap.

3 Cast off and work the other armhole to match.

4 Sew the shoulder straps to the back ends of the cast-off edge.

Visor

Headband

Cast on 40 sts in white.

rows 1–2: SS.

rows 3–5: knit.

rows 6–7: SS, beg with P row. Cast off purlwise.

Shade

Cast on 20 sts in white.

rows 1–2: SS.

rows 3–8: dec at both ends of every row.

rows 9–14: inc at both ends of every row.

rows 15–16: SS. Cast off.

Making up

1 Sew the row ends of the headband together, then fold it in half along the reverse ridge.

2 Oversew the cast-on and cast-off edges together.

3 Fold the shade in half, sew up the side seams.

4 Oversew the cast-on and cast-off edges together.

5 Stitch the shade to the bottom edge of the headband, with the seam at the back.

Racquet

Cast on 7 sts in black.

rows 1–10: change to light brown yarn, SS.

rows 11–20: SS.

row 21: skpo, K to last 2 sts, K2tog.

rows 22–76: beg with P row, SS (or until knitting fits around the loop from the dec row). Cast off.

You will need

Needles 3mm (US 3)

Yarns 50g balls of DK yarn in pink, white and brown

Small amounts of DK yarn in aqua, yellow and black; and 4-ply yarn in tan

Sewing needle and thread

Toy stuffing

Making up

1 Cut a straight straw to 5cm (2in) in length.

2 Cut a piece of plastic to 0.5cm (¼in) wide and 20cm (7¾in) in length. Trim away half of the width 3cm (1⅛in) from each end.

3 Place both trimmed-down ends of the plastic strip inside one end of the straw, leaving a 14cm (5½in) loop showing.

4 Sew up the black part of handle. Insert the straw and wrap the rest of the knitting around the loop.

5 Continue to sew knitting around the straw, then around the loop. Stitch the cast-off edge to the top of the handle.

6 For the mesh, use a single strand from the yarn used to knit racquet if it is strong enough. If not, use thick sewing thread instead. Make eight evenly-spaced vertical lines then weave ten rows horizontally through them.

Ball

Cast on 4 sts in yellow.

row 1: purl.

row 2: inc in every st.

rows 3–7: SS.

row 8: K2tog to end.

Break yarn and thread through sts.

Making up

1 Sew the seam to halfway and stuff firmly.

2 Sew up the rest of the seam.

With a smashing serve and a great backhand, Molly Mayberry is impatient for you to string her racquet so she can take on the competition.

Beach Volleyball

You will need

Needles 3mm (US 3)

Yarns 50g balls of DK yarn in caramel, cream, coral and pearl
Small amount of DK yarn in yellow

Sewing needle and thread

Toy stuffing

Athlete

1 Make a female figure in caramel, with knickers in pearl, and hair made from cream brushed DK yarn.

2 Lay strands of cream yarn across the top of the head, then use the same yarn to stitch them down two or three at a time with back stitch. Trim the hair to the same level all round.

Swimsuit

Bikini top

Cast on 18 sts in pink.

rows 1–2: SS.

rows 3–4: cast off 2 sts at beg of each row.

row 5: skpo, K to last 2 sts, K2tog.

row 6: purl.

rows 7–8: rep rows 5 and 6.

rows 9–10: SS.

row 11: K2, cast off 6, K1.

rows 12–22: work on 2sts only, SS, beg with a P row. Break yarn.

rows 12–22: return to the 2 sts left over and rep rows 12–22 above on these sts.

row 23: turn and cast on 6 sts.

Next row: K across 6 cast-on sts and the 2 sts just worked.

Next row: turn, cast on 2 sts purlwise, turn, K2 left from before.

Next row: turn, cast on 6 sts.

Next 4 rows: SS, beg with P row.

Cast off purlwise.

Bikini bottoms

Cast on 18 sts in pink.

rows 1–4: SS.

row 5: skpo, K to last 2 sts, K2tog.

row 6: P2 tog, P to last 2 sts, P2 tbl.

rows 7–12: rep rows 5 and 6 three times.

rows 13–18: SS.

rows 19–26: inc each end of every row.

rows 27–30: SS.

Cast off.

Making up

1 Sew up the side seams of the bikini bottoms.

2 Sew up the side seams of the bikini top.

Cap

Main cap

Cast on 38sts in white.

rows 1–2: knit.

rows 3–11: beg with P row, work SS.

row 12: (K4, K2tog) to last 2 sts, K2.

row 13: purl.

row 14: (K3, K2tog) to last 2 sts, K2.

row 15: purl.

row 16: (K2, K2tog) to last 2 sts, K2.

Break yarn and thread through rem sts.

Peak

Follow the instructions for the visor shade on page 18.

Making up

1 Sew up the back seam of the main cap.

2 Fold the visor in half, cast-on and cast-off edges together, and sew the sides together.

3 Cut a piece of plastic or card slightly smaller than the peak and insert it.

4 Oversew the open edge.

5 Stitch the peak to the bottom edge of the main cap, making sure that the seam of the cap is at the back.

Volleyball

Follow the instructions for the football on page 16, working in two row stripes of yellow and coral throughout.

Sigrid Sorenssen is the number one volleyball player on the beach – and the favourite of a lot of the other athletes!

Fencing

Athlete

1 Make a male figure with white feet and using white for rows 1–42 of the legs and torso.
2 Change to pink and continue from row 42.
3 Make the rest of the body as normal, with the hair base in grey.

Shoes

Make two, following the instructions for trainers on page 12, using grey for the uppers and soles, and white for the laces.

Jacket

Torso

Cast on 2 sts in white.
rows 1–2: SS.
row 3: inc in both sts.
row 4: purl.
row 5: inc 1 st at both ends.
row 6: purl.
rows 7–18: rep rows 5 and 6 six times.
rows 19–20: cast on 10 sts at beg of each row.
rows 21–28: SS.
row 29: K8, cast off 4 sts (1 st rem), K13 (14 sts on needle), cast off 4 sts, K7 (8 sts on needle). Work on these 8 sts only to end.
row 30: P8.
row 31: skpo, K to end.
row 32: purl.
rows 33–36: rep rows 31 and 32 twice.
rows 37–42: SS. Break yarn.
With wrong side facing, work on last 8 sts.
next row: purl.
next row: K to last 2 sts, K2tog.
next 6 rows: rep last two rows three times.
next 7 rows: SS. Cast off.
With wrong side facing, work on centre 14 sts.
next row: purl.
next row: skpo, K to last 2 sts, K2tog.
next 4 rows: rep last two rows twice more.
next row: purl.

next 2 rows: SS.
next row: K3, cast off 2 sts, k2.
next row: P3.
next row: K1, K2tog.
next row: P2.
next row: K2tog, fasten off.
Rejoin the yarn to remaining 3 sts and work to match the other side, reversing shaping.

Collar

Cast on 24 sts in white.
rows 1–2: SS.
rows 3–5: GS.
rows 6–7: SS.
Cast off purlwise.

Sleeves

Make two. Cast on 17 sts in white.
rows 1–6: SS.
row 7: inc 1 st each end of row.
rows 8–12: SS.
rows 13–18: rep rows 7–12.
rows 19–20: cast off 2 sts at beg of each row.
row 21: skpo, K to last 2 sts, K2tog.
row 22: purl.
rows 23–26: rep rows 21 and 22 twice more.
Cast off.

Making up

1 Along the back edge of the jacket torso, pick up and knit 13 sts evenly. Cast off purlwise.
2 Work the other edge in the same way.
3 Sew up the shoulder seam.
4 Sew the top of the sleeves into the armholes, then sew up the side and sleeve seams.
5 Stitch 1.5cm (½in) of the white elastic to the bottom edge of the jacket torso, inside the right back part. Stitch the other end to the inside front point.
6 Fold the collar in half and sew the edges together, then sew the cast-on and cast-off edges along the bottom together.

You will need

Needles 3mm (US 3)

Yarns 50g balls of DK yarn in white and pink

Small amounts of DK yarn in black and grey

Sewing needle and thread

Toy stuffing

Thin piece of clear plastic shaped to a point at one end

14 x 2.5cm (5½ x 1in) curved piece of plastic, such as the side of a yoghurt pot

7cm (2¾in) lengths of 0.5cm (¼in) wide elastic in black and white

7.5cm (3in) wide black sheer voile ribbon

7 Sew the collar on to the jacket. Sew three press studs on to the back opening, ensuring they are evenly placed.

Breeches

Make two. Cast on 18 sts in white.
rows 1–2: SS.
row 3: K5, M1, K8, M1, K5.
rows 4–12: SS.
row 13: K5, M1, K10, M1, K5.
rows 14–16: SS.
rows 17–18: cast off 2 sts at beg of next 2 rows.
rows 19–30: SS.
row 31: cast off 4 sts, K1 (2 sts on needle). Cast off to end.
Return to the 2 sts left over and GS 34 rows to make the shoulder strap.
Cast off.

Making up

1 Sew up the leg seams then sew the two pieces together.
2 Sew the cast-off end of the shoulder straps to the opposite side of the waist. Make sure not to let them twist.

Baron von Baumwolle is a deadly opponent to face with a blade – but jolly friendly over a nice cup of tea.

In order to stop the figure being too bulky, the fencer's leggings are knitted into the athlete's body from the start.

Foil

Cast on 10 sts in grey.
row 1: inc in every st.
rows 2–16: SS.
row 17: K2tog to end.
row 18: P2tog to end.
rows 19–24: SS on the 5 rem sts.
Cast off.

Making up

1 Sew the work together along the row ends.
2 Fold the piece in half so that the cast-on edge meets the first decrease row.
3 Trim the plastic into a blade, such that the blunt end is small enough to fit inside the knitted handle (the last six rows worked).
4 Gather the cast-on edge tightly and stitch through both layers of knitting. This is the hand guard of the foil.

Mask

Upper head guard

Cast on 32 sts in black.
rows 1–4: SS.
rows 5–7: knit.
rows 8–11: SS beg with P row.
Cast off purlwise.

Neck guard

Cast on 22 sts in white.
rows 1–4: SS.
rows 5–12: dec 1 st at each end of every row.
Cast off.

Making up

1 Fold the upper head guard in half. Stitch the cast-on and cast-off edges together. Insert the curved piece of plastic and sew up the open ends.
2 Fold the voile ribbon in half, turn over the raw edge and gather. Place it along the inside edge of the upper head guard centred at the top, then stitch it in place.
3 Sew the sides of the ribbon down inside the front edges of the upper head guard, ending at the bottom edge.
4 Stitch the white neck guard to the bottom of the upper head guard, attaching it to the ribbon on the front and along the knitting on the sides.
5 Use the needle and thread to attach the black elastic around the back of the head, 1cm (½in) up from the bottom of the mask.

The rear of the mask.

Hurdling

Athlete

1 Make a female figure in brown with underwear in lilac, and hair base made from doubled dark brown 4-ply yarn.
2 Knot 20cm (8in) strands of dark brown yarn all round the cast-on edge by folding them in half and pushing the loops through the stitches.
3 Pull the cut ends through and pull tight.
4 Pull the hair up into a pony tail. For a frizzy look, ruffle the pony tail a little.

Trainers

Make two, following the instructions for trainers (see page 12), using white for the uppers, soles and laces.

Top

Make one, following the instructions for the bikini top (see page 20) in lime green.

Shorts

Make two. Cast on 26 sts in lime green.
rows 1–2: SS.
rows 3–4: Cast off 2 sts at beg of next 2 rows.
row 5: skpo, K to last 2 sts, K2tog.
row 6: purl.
rows 7–8: rep rows 5 and 6.
rows 9–12: SS.
Cast off.

Making up

1 Fold the leg piece in half and sew the row ends together.
2 Sew the leg pieces together from the cast-off sts to the waist.

Hurdle

Base

With white yarn cast on 7 sts.
Work SS until work measures 40cm (15¾in).
Cast off.

Posts

Make two. Cast on 7 sts in blue.
Work SS until work measures 12cm (4¾in).
Cut yarn and thread through sts.

Bar

With red yarn cast on 32 sts.
rows 1–4: SS.
rows 5–6: knit.
rows 7–10: SS.
Cast off purlwise.

Making up

1 Cut two drinking straws to 20cm (8in) in length from the top. Roll up the paper firmly and join the straws at the ends nearest the bends by putting the rolled-up paper inside and closing the gap, securing with sticky tape.
2 Bend the straws, the same distance along, at the other ends. Insert more rolled-up scrap paper and secure with sticky tape, making a rectangle.
3 Sew the cast-on and cast-off edges of the base together. Place the knitting round the straws and slip stitch the row ends together all the way round.
4 Cut a straw to 11cm (4¼in) in length from the bottom. Wrap one of the post pieces round the straw and sew up the seam.
5 Sew one post to each corner of one of the base's long sides.
6 Fold the bar piece in half along the turning ridge and sew the ends together. Insert the plastic piece, then oversew the cast-on and cast-off edges together.
7 Attach the bar to the posts by sewing 0.5cm (¼in) down at each edge.

Leaping gracefully over the final hurdle, Amaka Omiata is not racing yet – she has just realised she is running late for the bus.

Field Hockey

Athlete

1 Make a female figure in brown with underwear in peach, and hair base made from dark brown.

2 Knot 20cm (8in) strands of dark brown yarn all round the cast-on edge by folding them in half and pushing the loops through the stitches.

3 Pull the cut ends through, pull tight then take them into a pony tail at the top of the head. Tie a piece of wool tightly round the pony tail and fasten off.

Boots

Make two, following the instructions for trainers (see page 12), using black for the uppers, soles and laces.

Skirt

Cast on 50sts in lime green.
Change colour to maroon.
rows 1–8: SS.
row 9: (K4, K2tog) to last 2 sts, K2.
rows 10–16: SS, beg with P row.
row 17: (K3, K2tog) to last 2 sts, K2.
rows 18–20: SS, beg with P row. Cast off.
With green and right side facing, pick up and knit 15 sts along row ends.
Cast off purlwise.
Work the other edge in the same way.

Making up

1 Stitch a press stud on to the skirt at the top, overlapping the skirt on the left side. Make sure to wrap it firmly enough for the skirt not to fall down.

Top

Back

Cast on 22 sts in maroon.
rows 1–8: SS.
rows 9–10: change to lime green, SS.

rows 11–12: change to maroon, SS.
rows 13–14: change to lime green, SS.
rows 15–16: change to maroon, SS, casting off 2 sts at beg of each row.
row 17: skpo, K to last 2 sts, K2tog.
row 18: purl.
rows 19–26: rep rows 17 and 18 four times. Cast off.

Front

Follow the instructions for the back of the top until row 16.
row 17: skpo, K7, turn.
row 18: purl.
rows 19–26: rep rows 17 and 18 four times. Leave sts on holder. Work other side to match, reversing shaping.

Sleeves

Cast on 18 sts in lime green.
rows 1–8: SS.
rows 9–10: cast off 2 sts at beg of each row.
row 11: skpo, K to last 2 sts, K2tog.
row 12: purl.
rows 13–20: rep rows 11 and 12 four times. Cast off.

Making up

1 Make the neck edge as follows: using lime green and with the right side facing, knit 4 sts from right front, pick up 4 sts from top of sleeve, 8 sts from back, 4 sts from top of other sleeve and knit 4 sts from left front. Cast off purlwise.
2 Sew raglan seams.
3 Sew sleeve and side seams.

You will need

Needles 3mm (US 3)

Yarns 50g balls of DK yarn in brown, maroon and lime green
Small amounts of DK yarn in black, light beige, peach and dark brown.
Sewing needle and thread
Toy stuffing
One drinking straw
Piece of hard cardboard or plastic

Hockey stick

Cast on 8 sts in black.
rows 1–12: SS.
rows 13–18: change colour to beige, SS.
row 19: K3, M1, K4, M1, K1.
rows 20–42: SS.
row 43: skpo, K to last 2 sts, K2tog.
row 44: purl.
rows 45–46: rep rows 43 and 44 once more. Cast off.

Making up

1 Using the template below, cut the shape of the hockey stick from hard cardboard or plastic.
2 Cut a 2cm (¾in) long piece of drinking straw. Push the straw on to the end without the curve, for the handle.
3 Wrap the hockey stick knitting round the plastic shape and sew the seam down the inside edge.

The template for the hockey stick, reproduced at actual size.

Plucky Pippa Pickpepper is ready to bully off. If you would prefer her to have some shorts to wear (as in the picture on the middle left), follow the instructions on page 14, using maroon yarn.

Karate

Athlete

Make a male figure in beige with underpants in white, and hair base made from black fun fur.

Jacket

Cast on 80 sts in white.
row 1: knit.
row 2: K2, skpo, K to last 4 sts, K2tog, K2.
row 3: K2, P to last 2 sts, K2.
rows 4–15: rep rows 2 and 3 six times.
row 16: K2, skpo, K18. Turn.
row 17: Cast off 2 sts purlwise, P to last 4 st, P2tog, tbl, K2.
row 18: K2, skpo, K to end.
row 19: purl to last 4 sts, P2tog, tbl, K2.
rows 20–29: rep rows 18 and 19 five times.
Cast off.
Rejoin wool to remaining sts and cast off 2 sts.
next row: K until there are 18 sts on needle. Cast off 4sts, K to the last 4 sts, K2tog, K2. Put 18 centre sts on a holder.
next row: K2, P2tog, P to end.
next row: K to last 4 sts, K2tog, K2.
next row: rep last two rows until 4 sts remain. Cast off. Break yarn.
Rejoin yarn to sts left with wrong side facing
next 15 rows: beg with P row, work SS.
Cast off.

Sleeves

Make two. Cast on 22 sts in white.
row 1: knit.
rows 2–17: SS.
rows 18–19: Cast off 2 sts at beg of each row.
row 20: skpo, K to last 2sts, K2tog.
row 21: purl.
Cast off.

Trousers

Legs

Make two. Cast on 26 sts in white.
rows 1–24: SS.
rows 25–26: Cast off 2 sts at beg of each row.
row 27: skpo, K to last 2 sts, K2tog.
rows 28–38: SS beg with P row.
Cast off.

Making up

1 Sew up the shoulder seams of the jacket.
2 Sew up the seams of the sleeves, then sew the sleeves into the armhole openings.
3 Sew up the leg seams. Sew in all yarn ends.

Black belt

Cast on 3 sts in black.
rows 1–60: GS.
Cast off.

You will need

Needles 3mm (US 3)
Yarns 50g balls of DK yarn in beige, white and black
50g ball of matt cotton in white
Small amount of black fun fur
Sewing needle and thread
Toy stuffing

Tatsuo Ryukyu is friendly and chatty – in between bouts, he loves to spin yarns about his days at the Dojo.

Rhythmic Gymnastics

You will need

Needles 3mm (US 3)

Yarns 50g ball of DK yarn in dark brown
50g ball of 3-ply yarn in metallic silver
Small amount of DK yarn in black
Sewing needle and thread
Toy stuffing
50cm (19¾in) silver bead chain trim
Two thick pipe cleaners
Two small press studs

Athlete

1 Make a female figure in dark brown with hair base made from black.
2 To achieve the curled effect, pull out some spare knitting (the tension square previously worked is a good source).
3 Pile the pulled-out knitting on to the top of the hairpiece and stitch it in place, allowing the curls to be longer at the back.
4 Wrap silver beading around the hair four times and stitch in place with black thread.

Leotard

Cast on 11 sts in doubled silver yarn.
rows 1–8: SS.
row 9: dec 1st at both ends.
row 10: purl.
rows 11–16: rep rows 9 and 10 three times.
rows 17–20: SS.
row 21: inc 1 st at beg and end of row.
row 22: purl.
rows 23–28: rep rows 21 and 22 three times.
rows 29–32: SS.
row 33: inc at beg and end of row.
row 34: purl.
rows 35–44: K3, cast off 7 sts, K to end.
rows 45–50: SS on last 3 sts.
Cast off.
Rejoin yarn to rem 3 sts and work to match.

Making up

1 Stitch the four SS rows at each side of the leotard together for the side seams.
2 Sew one part of a press stud to the underside at the end of the shoulder strap, and the receiving part to the back where they meet.
3 Repeat on the other side.

Shoes

Make two. Cast on 20 sts in doubled silver yarn.
rows 1–4: SS.
row 5: K3, skpo, K2tog, K6, skpo, K2tog, K3.
row 6: purl.
row 7: K2, skpo, K2tog, K4, skpo, K2tog, K2.
row 8: purl. Cast off.

Ties

Make four. Cast on 30 sts in brown DK yarn.
Cast off all sts.

Making up

1 Sew the seam along the row ends and take it under the foot. Sew the toe seam at the cast-off end.
2 Stitch a tie to each side of the shoe at the cast-on edge. Wrap them around the ankle and tie it at the back of the leg.

Ball

Follow the instructions for the football on page 16, working in double metallic yarn.

Hoop

Cast on 7 sts with doubled silver yarn.
SS until work is long enough to wrap round hoop. Cast off.

Making up

1 Make a circle with two thick pipe cleaners, the joins opposite each other for strength. Wrap the circle with yarn to keep them together.
2 Sew the cast-on and cast-off edges of the hoop work together. Place it round the outside edge of the hoop and stitch it in place, hiding the seam in the centre of the hoop so that it is less visible.

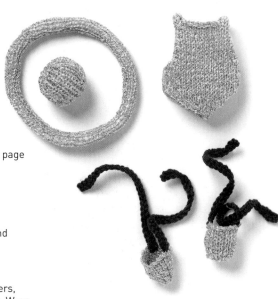

Gymnastics requires strength, coordination and grace: qualities Lydia Taylor possesses in abundance. By virtue of being made from wool, she is also very flexible!

Dressage

Athlete

1 Make a female figure in light beige with underwear in lilac, and hair base made from yellow.
2 Follow step 2 of the instructions for the long hair from the tennis player (see page 18), using yellow.
3 Tie the hair into a pony tail at the back of the neck.

Coat

Back

Cast on 11 sts in black.
rows 1–16: SS.
Make another the same, do not break yarn.
rows 17–32: SS across all sts.
rows 33–34: Cast off 2 sts at beg of each row.
row 35: skpo, K to last 2 sts, K2tog.
row 36: purl.
rows 37–40: rep rows 35 and 36 twice more.
rows 41–46: SS. Cast off.

Front right side

Cast on 18 sts in black.
rows 1–15: SS.
row 16: Cast off 2 sts purlwise, P to end.
row 17: skpo, K to end.
row 18: P2tog, P to last 2 sts, P2tog, tbl.
rows 19–20: rep rows 17 and 18.
row 21: as row 17.
row 22: P to last 2 sts, P2tog tbl.
rows 23–30: rep rows 21 and 22 three times. Cast off.

Front left side

Work as front right side to row 15.
row 16: purl.
row 17: cast off 2 sts, K to end.
row 18: P2tog, P to end.
row 19: skpo, K last 2 sts, K2tog.
rows 20–21: rep rows 18 and 19.
row 22: P2tog, p to end.

row 23: K to last 2 sts, K2tog.
rows 24–29: rep rows 22 and 23 three times.
row 30: purl. Cast off.

Sleeves

Cast on 18 sts in black.
rows 1–10: SS.
row 11: inc 1 st at both ends of row.
rows 12–18: SS, beg with P row.
rows 19–20: Cast off 2 sts at beg of each row.
row 21: skpo, K to last 2 sts, K2tog.
row 22: purl.
rows 23–24: rep rows 21 and 22. Cast off.

Making up

1 Sew up the shoulder seams. Sew the sleeve tops into the armholes. Sew up the side and sleeve seams.
2 Stitch two small gold beads to the back of the coat, 1cm (½in) up from where the tails join and three rows apart.
3 Stitch two rows of three beads to the right front part of the jacket.
4 Sew two small black press studs inside the front edge of the coat, one at bottom corner of right front and another at start of front shaping.

Cravat

Cast on 12 sts in white 4-ply yarn.
rows 1–12: SS.
row 13: K2tog to end.
row 14: P2tog to end.
rows 15–44: SS.
rows 45–46: inc in every st.
rows 47–58: SS.
Cast off.
Sew small bead to centre of the eighth row.

You will need

Needles 3mm (US 3)

Yarns 50g balls of DK yarn in light beige, black and white
50g ball of 4-ply yarn in white
Small amounts of DK yarn in yellow and lilac

Sewing needle and thread

Toy stuffing

Nine small gold beads

Small cardboard ring to fit inside hat

Boots

Make two. Cast on 14 sts in black.
row 1: purl.
row 2: inc in every st.
rows 3–13: SS, beg with P row.
row 14: K8, cast off 12, K to end.
row 15: P8, close the gap between st groups by pushing the sts together, P8.
rows 16–19: SS.
row 20: inc at both ends of row.
rows 21–25: SS.
row 26: As row 20.
rows 27–29: SS. Cast off.

Making up

1 Sew the top of the boot opening closed.
2 Stitch the back seam and sole seam.

Jodhpurs

Make two. With white cast on 20 sts.
rows 1–12: SS.
row 13: inc 1, K to end, inc 1.
rows 14–20: SS beg with P row.
rows 21–22: cast off 2 sts at beg of each row.
row 23: skpo, K to last 2 sts, K2tog.
rows 24–34: SS, beg with P row
Cast off

Making up

1 Sew up the leg seam on each piece.
2 Sew the two pieces together. When fitting the jodhpurs on the figure, pull the boots up over the cast-on edge.

Dressage looks very elegant, and takes a great deal of skill. It is not all glamour though: Katie has to muck out the stables herself.

Hat

Side

Cast on 38 sts in black.
rows 1–6: SS.
Cast off.

Top

Cast on 4 sts in black.
row 1: purl.
row 2: inc 1 st at both ends of row.
rows 3–8: rep rows 1 and 2 three times.
rows 9–11: SS.
row 12: skpo, K to last 2 sts.
row 13: purl.
rows 14–19: rep rows 12 and 13 three times.
Cast off.

Brim

Cast on 38 sts in black.
row 1: purl.
row 2: (K1, inc1) to end.
rows 3–4: SS beg with P row.
rows 5–6: knit.
rows 7–8: SS beg with P row.
row 9: (P1, P2tog) to end.
Cast off.

Making up

1 Sew up the back seam of the side piece.
2 Sew the top to the side all the way round.
3 Sew the row ends of the brim together, then fold along the reverse ridge row.
4 Stitch the cast-on and cast-off edges of the brim together, then place round the bottom of the side piece and oversew on the wrong side.
5 Place the cardboard ring high inside the top of the hat.
6 Stitch the completed hat to the top of the doll's head.

White Water Rafting

Athlete

Make a male figure in light brown with underpants in white, and hair base made from blond fun fur.

Shorts

Make a pair of shorts following the instructions on page 14, using white yarn.

Top

Make a top following the instructions for the shirt on page 16, using light blue yarn.

Kayak

Bottom

Cast on 3 sts in royal blue.
row 1: inc in first and last st.
row 2: P2, slip 1 purlwise, P2.
row 3: K1, inc 1, K centre st, inc 1, K1.
row 4: P to centre st, slip it, P to end.
next rows: Continue in this way increasing each side of centre st on right side, and slipping the centre st on P rows with yarn held in front, until there are 37 sts.
next rows: Continue without increasing until work measures 25cm (10in), still slipping the centre P st on each P row.
next row: K16, skpo, K1, K2tog, K16.
next row: P to centre st , slip, P to end.
next rows: Continue dec in this way until 3 sts remain.
next row: Slip 1, K2tog, psso.
Fasten off.

Top

Cast on 2 sts in white.
row 1: inc in both sts.
row 2: purl.
row 3: inc in first and last st of row.
rows 4–5: rep rows 2 and 3.
rows 6–20: SS, beg with P row.
row 21: as row 3.
rows 22–28: SS, beg with P row.
rows 29–52: rep rows 22–28 three times.
row 53: as row 3.
rows 54–56: SS.
row 57: inc 1, K3, cast off 10, K2, inc1.
Turn and work on 5 sts just worked only.
rows 58–70: SS.
Return to remaining 5 sts.
With wrong side facing, and beg with P row, SS 13 rows.
row 71: K across 5 sts, turn, cast on 10 sts, turn, K across 5 sts left.
row 72: purl.
row 73: skpo, K to last 2 sts, K2tog.
rows 74–80: SS.
rows 81–104: rep rows 73–80 three times.
row 105: rep row 73.
rows 106–120: SS.
row 121: rep row 73.
row 122: purl.
rows 123–128: rep rows 121 and 122 three times.
K2tog. Break yarn, fasten off.

Lining

Cast on 20 sts in cream.
row 1: purl.
row 2: inc in every st.
rows 3–21: SS.
row 22: inc 4 sts evenly across row.

rows 23–49: SS.
rows 50–55: change to black yarn, SS.
row 56: K7, cast off 8 sts, K13 [14 on needle], cast off 8 sts, K to end.
row 57: working on last 7 sts only, P.
row 58: skpo, K5.
rows 59–62: rep rows 57 and 58 twice more.
row 63: purl. Cast off.
Return to 14 sts left. With wrong side facing, rejoin black.
row 57: purl.
row 58: skpo, K to last 2 sts, K2tog.
rows 59–62: rep rows 57 and 58 twice more.
row 63: purl. Cast off.

Making up

1 Sew the top of the kayak to the bottom of the kayak all round.

2 Stuff the kayak with toy stuffing firmly at the points. Leave room for the athlete to sit with his legs in the lining.

3 Mark the centre point of the cast-on edge of the lining, then fold the side edges in so that the bottom corners meet at this point. Pin together and sew up.

4 Sew up the lining seam, making sure that the area where the colour changes from cream to black match up for the overlap cover.

5 Put the lining inside the kayak with the right side of the work visible.

6 Turn down the extension pieces of the black to form the protection cover and slip stitch it to the top of kayak.

You will need

Needles 3mm (US 3)
Yarns 50g balls of DK yarn in light brown, pale blue, white, royal blue, cream and black
Small amount of blond fun fur
Sewing needle and thread
Toy stuffing
Straight drinking straw
Sturdy plastic

Posing with his kayak is something Brad does very well – he practises it more than his safety procedures!

Paddle

Shaft

Cast on 7 sts in black.
Work SS to slightly less than 13cm (5in).

Paddles

Make two. Cast on 4 sts in black.
rows 1–2: SS.
row 3: inc 1 st at both ends.
row 4: purl.
rows 5–8: rep rows 3 and 4.
rows 9–20: SS.
row 21: skpo, K to last 2 sts, K2tog.
row 22: purl.
rows 23–24: rep rows 21 and 22.
row 25: inc both ends of row.
row 26: purl.
rows 27–28: rep rows 25 and 26.
rows 29–40: SS.
row 41: skpo, K to last 2 sts, K2tog.
row 42: purl.
rows 43–46: rep rows 41 and 42 twice more.
rows 47–48: SS.
Cast off.

Making up

1 Cut a drinking straw to 16cm (6¼in) in length.
2 Use the template to cut two paddle shapes out of plastic.
3 Cut two 1.5cm (½in) long slits on each side of the straw. Insert the paddle shape and stick it down securely with sticky tape. Do the same at the other end of the straw, making sure the paddles are facing the same way.
4 Place the shaft knitting round the straw and sew up the seam.
5 Sew up one side seam of each paddle. Slip them over the plastic shapes on the straw, then sew up the other sides.
6 Sew the paddles to the knitting at the end of the shaft.

Crash helmet

Cast on 42 sts in yellow.
rows 1–8: SS.
row 9: (K4, K2tog) to end.
row 10 and all subsequent even rows: purl.
row 11: (K3, K2tog) to end.
row 13: (K2, K2tog) to end.
row 15: (K1, K2tog) to end.
row 17: K2tog to end, break yarn and thread through all sts.

Ear flaps

With right side of work facing at cast-on edge, starting at seventh st from the edge of the right-hand side, pick up and knit 5 sts.
rows 1–3: beg with P row, SS.
row 4: skpo, K2, K2tog.
row 5: purl.
row 6: sl1, K2tog, psso.
Fasten off.
Make another in the same way, but start by picking up sts from the eleventh st from the edge of the left-hand side.

Chin strap

Cast on 2 sts.
rows 1–16: GS.
Cast off.

Making up

1 Sew up the back seam of the crash helmet, from the gathered stitches at the top down to the cast-on edge.
2 Sew the point of each ear flap to each end of the chin strap, making sure not to twist it.

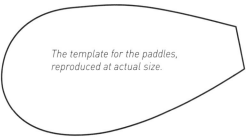

The template for the paddles, reproduced at actual size.

Ice Skating

Athlete

1 Make a female figure in pink with hair base in yellow.

2 Follow step 2 of the instructions for the long hair from the tennis player (see page 18), using yellow DK yarn.

3 Pull all the strands up into a pony tail and secure it tightly. Curl the remaining length of hair round a finger, tuck in the ends and then stitch them to the head with matching yarn.

Costume

Make the main part of the costume following the instructions for the leotard on page 32, using doubled metallic red yarn.

Skirt

Cast on 80 sts in single metallic red yarn.

rows 1–12: SS.

row 13: K2tog to end.

row 14: purl. Cast off.

Making up

The skirt will need blocking to stop it curling up.

1 Sew up back seam of skirt.

2 Place the skirt on the main part of the costume and pin along the first row above the leg shaping and side seams. Stitch it into place.

Ice skates

Make two, following the instructions for trainers (see page 12), using doubled metallic red yarn for the uppers, soles and laces.

Blade

Make two. Cast on 6 sts in doubled metallic silver yarn.

rows 1–2: SS.

rows 3–4: cast on 3 sts at beg of each row.

rows 5–6: SS.

rows 7–8: cast off 3 sts at beg of each row.

rows 9–18: SS. Cast off.

Making up

1 Use the template to cut a blade out of thick plastic.

2 Fold the blade work in half lengthways, insert plastic shape and stitch closed all round.

3 Make a second blade in the same way, then sew one blade to the bottom of each boot as shown in the picture.

Hairband

Cast on 6 sts in doubled metallic red yarn. Work in SS until piece fits around bottom of hair bun when slightly stretched.

Cast off and sew cast-on and cast-off edges together in place.

Flower

Cast on 12 sts in metallic red yarn.

row 1: inc in every st.

row 2: knit.

row 3: purl.

row 4: cast off 2 sts, then put 1 st from right-hand needle back on to the left needle. Cast on 2 sts. Cast off 4 sts. Rep until all the sts have been used up (this gives a picot edge).

Making up

1 Holding the centre firmly and keeping work flat, coil the work round so that the flower has a double layer.

2 Stitch through the centre layers to hold the flower in position.

3 Stitch three gold beads in the centre of the flower, then sew it to the hairband slightly off-centre.

The template for the ice skate blades, reproduced at actual size.

You will need

Needles 3mm (US 3)

Yarns 50g balls of DK yarn in pink and yellow

50g balls of 3-ply yarn in metallic red and metallic silver

Sewing needle and thread

Toy stuffing

Sturdy plastic

Three gold beads

Bridgit Kurgerplatz is the picture of elegance on the ice in her smart costume and matching boots. The picture below shows the join between the leotard and the skirt, and also the fastenings of the costume.

Skiing

Athlete

Make a female figure in light brown, with hair base in cream.

Ski boots

Make two, following the instructions for trainers on page 12. Use black for the uppers, soles and laces.

Crash helmet

Make one, following the instructions for the crash helmet on page 41, using white yarn.

Bodysuit

Cast on 20 sts in blue.
rows 1–28: SS.
row 29: K1, M1, K to last st, M1, K1.
rows 30–34: SS, break yarn.
Make another leg in the same way up to row 7.
row 7: K to last st with blue, K1 in light blue.
row 8: P2 in light blue, work the rest of the row in blue.
rows 9–34: continue in this way, working in SS, and with 1 more st in light blue on every row.
When row 34 is completed, start to work across both sets of sts as follows:
rows 35–50: SS.
row 51: K11, cast off 4, K13 [14 on needle], cast off 4, K to end.
row 52: P on last 11 sts.
row 53: skpo, K to end.
rows 54–59: rep rows 52 and 53 three times.
row 60: purl. Cast off.
Transfer the other set of 11 sts on to a needle, beg with wrong side facing.
row 52: purl.
row 53: K to last 2 sts, K2tog.
rows 54–59: rep rows 52 and 53 three times.
row 60: purl.
Cast off. Put centre 14 sts on a needle.
rows 61–69: with wrong side facing, beg with P row, work SS.

row 70: K3, cast off 8 sts, K2.
rows 71–75: SS.
Cast off. Return to last 3 sts.
rows 71–75: beg with p row, work SS. Cast off.

Making up

1 Join the leg seams.
2 Join the back seam.
3 Sew press studs on to the shoulder straps and back, making sure the straps will fit when they are closed.

Jacket

Back

Cast on 22 sts in blue.
rows 1–6: SS.
rows 7–8: Cast off 2 sts at beg of each row.
row 9: skpo, K to last 2 sts, K2tog.
row 10: purl.
rows 11–12: rep rows 9 and 10.
rows 13–24: SS. Cast off.

Front left side

Cast on 18 sts in blue.
rows 1–7: SS.
row 8: Cast off 2 sts purlwise, P to end.
row 9: K to last 2 sts, K2tog.
row 10: purl.
rows 11–12: rep rows 9 and 10.
rows 13–18: SS.
row 19: K4, cast off 6 sts, K to end.
row 20: purl.
row 21: skpo, K2.
row 22: purl. Cast off. Break off yarn.
Rejoin yarn to remaining 4 sts.
row 20: purl.
row 21: K2, K2tog.
row 22: purl. Cast off.

Front right side

Cast on 6 sts in blue.
rows 1–6: SS.
row 7: cast off 2 sts at beg of row.

row 8: purl.
row 9: skpo, K to end.
rows 10–11: rep rows 8 and 9.
rows 12–22: SS. Cast off.

Left sleeve

Cast on 20 sts in blue.
rows 1–20: SS.
rows 21–22: cast off 2 sts at beg of each row.
row 23: skpo, K to last 2 sts, K2tog.
row 24: purl.
rows 25–26: rep rows 23 and 24. Cast off.

Right sleeve

Cast on 20 sts in blue.
rows 1–4: SS.
row 5: K19, change to light blue, K1.
row 6: P2, change to blue, P18.
Continue in this way, following the instructions for the left sleeve, and working 1 more st in contrast on every row until sleeve is finished.

Making up

1 Sew up the shoulder seams.
2 Pick up and K 16 sts down left front. Cast off purlwise.
3 Pick up with right side facing and K 3 sts down left front, 6 sts from cast off at front, 6 sts up right front, 10 sts from back, 16 sts from left front edge. Cast off purlwise.
4 Sew press studs to the front edge at the top and bottom of jacket opening.

You will need

Needles 3mm (US 3)
Yarns 50g balls of DK yarn in light brown, blue, light blue, black and white
Small amount of DK yarn in cream and yellow
Sewing needle and thread
Toy stuffing
Two small press studs
Stiff card
Straight drinking straws
2.5cm (1in) lengths of 0.5cm (¼in) wide elastic in black

Parvati Bhatt waves to the crowds after swishing to a halt at the end of the course. After a hard day's skiing, she will be ready for a nice cup of hot chocolate at the chalet.

Skis

Make two. Cast on 1 st in black.

row 1: inc 1.

row 2: inc 1 purlwise, P1.

row 3: inc 1 sts at both end of row.

next rows: rep rows 2 and 3 until you have 11 sts.

next rows: SS until work measures 28cm (11in) from start.

next 38 rows: change to light blue, SS.

next 20 rows: change to black, SS.

next 20 rows: change to white, SS.

next 4 rows: change to yellow, SS.

next row: skpo, K to last 2 sts, K2tog.

next row: purl.

next rows: rep last two rows until 3 sts remain. sl1, K1, psso, fasten off.

Making up

1 Fold the knitting in half, then sew up one side and the point.

2 Cut two pieces of stiff card, 28cm (11in) long and 4cm (1½in) wide. Cut points at one end and curve the card at the end upwards slightly.

3 Insert the cardboard into the knitting and stitch the other side up.

4 Use the needle and thread to attach black elastic halfway along each ski.

Ski poles

Make two. With black cast on 7 sts.

rows 1–35: SS.

Thread yarn through all sts and pull up tightly.

Making up

1 Cut a piece of straight drinking straw 12cm (4¾in) long.

2 Wrap the knitting around the straw and sew up the seam.

3 Close the gap at the bottom and sew up.

4 Make a handle by casting on 20 sts with black and casting all sts off. Stitch the ends together to make a loop.

5 Sew the handle to the top of the pole.

6 Make the second pole in the same way.

Archery

Athlete

1 Make a female figure in beige, with hair base in light brown and underwear in light purple.
2 Follow steps 2 and 3 of the instructions for the long hair from the athlete in training (see page 12), using light brown.
3 Unravel the strands of hair for a frizzy look.

Shoes

Make two, following the instructions for trainers on page 12. Use white for the uppers, soles and laces.

Skirt

Cast on 70 sts in white.
rows 1–2: SS.
row 3: K1, (yo, K2tog) to last st, K1.
rows 4–16: SS, beg with P row.
row 17: (K8, K2tog) to end.
rows 18–20: SS.
row 21: (K7, K2tog) to end.
rows 22–24: SS.
row 25: (K6, K2tog) to end.
rows 26–28: SS.
row 29: (K1, K2tog) to end.
row 30: purl. Cast off.

Making up

1 Sew up the back seam.
2 Turn up the hem to form the picot edge and slip stitch the cast-on edge in place.

Top

Back

Cast on 26 sts in white.
rows 1–4: K1, P1 (rib).
rows 5–12: SS.
rows 13–14: cast off 2 sts at beg of each row.
rows 15–26: SS. Cast off.

Left front

Cast on 13 sts in white.
rows 1–4: K1, P1 (rib)
rows 5–12: SS.
row 13: cast off 2 sts, K to end.
row 14: purl.
row 15: skpo, K to end.
rows 16–17: rep rows 14 and 15.
rows 18–19: SS.
row 20: cast off 3 sts purlwise, P to end.
row 21: K to last 2 sts, K2tog.
row 22: purl.
rows 23–26: rep rows 21 and 22 twice more.
Cast off.

Right front

Follow the instruction for the left front until row 11.
row 12: cast off 2 sts, P to end.
row 13: knit.
row 14: purl.
row 15: K to last 2 sts, K2tog.
rows 16–17: rep rows 14 and 15.
row 18: purl.
row 19: cast off 3 sts, K to end.
row 20: purl.
row 21: skpo, K to end.
row 22–25: rep rows 20 and 21 twice more.
row 26: purl.
Cast off.

Sleeves

Cast on 23 sts in white.
rows 1–4: K1, P1 (rib).
rows 5–10: SS.
rows 11–12: cast off 2 sts at beg of each row.
row 13: skpo, K to last 2 sts, K2tog.
row 14: purl.
rows 15–20: rep rows 13 and 14 three times.
Cast off.

You will need

Needles 3mm (US 3)

Yarns 50g balls of DK yarn in beige, light brown, pink and light purple
50g ball of white 4-ply cotton yarn
Small amount of DK yarn in brown

Toy stuffing
Sewing needle and thread
Two small press studs
Stiff card
Straight drinking straws
25 x 1.5cm (10 x ¾in) piece of plastic, ideally with a natural curve

Making up

1 Sew the left and right front parts to the back at the shoulders.
2 Pick up and knit 23 sts evenly for the neckband. Work K1, P1 (rib) for two rows, then cast off in rib.
3 Make the front bands: pick up and knit 13 sts along the front of the work: 1 row K1, P1 (rib), then cast off in rib. Work the other front part in the same way.
4 Sew the top of sleeve into the armhole. Sew up the sleeve and side seams.
5 Stitch three small press studs inside the area where the front parts overlap.

Arm protector

Cast on 14 sts in pink.
rows 1–10: SS.
Cast off.

Making up

1 Lace yarn through alternate row ends, working up and down the piece.
2 Tie the work in a bow when placed in position on the arm.

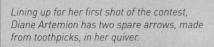

Lining up for her first shot of the contest, Diane Artemion has two spare arrows, made from toothpicks, in her quiver.

Hat

Side

Cast on 48 sts in pink.
rows 1–2: SS.
row 3: (K6, K2tog) to end.
row 4: purl.
row 5: (K5, K2tog) to end.
rows 6–10: SS.
Cast off.

Top

Cast on 3 sts.
row 1: inc in first and last st.
row 2: purl.
rows 3–8: rep rows 1 and 2 three times.
rows 9–10: SS.
row 11: skpo, K to last 2 sts, K2tog.
row 12: purl.
rows 13–18: rep rows 11 and 12 three times.
Cast off.

Making up

1 Sew up the back seam.
2 Sew the top on to the side piece.

Quiver

Pouch

Cast on 16 sts in brown.
rows 1–16: SS.
row 17: K1, M1, K7, M1, K8.
rows 18–23: SS, beg with P row.
rows 24–25: K.
Cast off knitwise.

Belt

Cast on 38 sts in brown. Cast off.

Making up

1 Fold the pouch in half so the two ends meet, then sew up the side and bottom seams.
2 Sew one end of the belt to the back of the pouch near the top.
3 Sew a press stud to the other end of the belt and position the receiving part of press stud on the back of the quiver. Make sure that the quiver is at hip level when the belt is positioned on the archer.

Bow

Cast on 8 sts in brown.
Work in SS until the piece is slightly shorter than the plastic.
Cast off.

Making up

1 Sew the ends closed, then place the knitting round the plastic and oversew it in place.
2 Add a string to the bow by stitching beige yarn 1cm (½in) in from the ends, bending the bow so that the yarn you are stitching with measures 15cm (6in).
3 Bend the ends of the bow at the bottom and the top so these parts recurve.

Chest protector

Cast on 12 sts in pink.
rows 1–2: SS.
row 3: K1, M1, K to last st, M1, K1.
rows 4–5: rep rows 2 and 3.
rows 6–8: beg with a P row, SS.
row 9: K4, cast off 4 sts, K to end.
rows 10–14: on last 8 sts, beg with P row, SS.
row 15: K to last 2 sts, K2tog.
row 16: purl.
row 17: skpo, K to end.
row 18: purl.
rows 19–22: rep rows 15–18.
rows 23–24: rep rows 15–16.
Cast off.
With right side facing, SS 4 rows on sts left.
next row: K2, K2tog.
next 7 rows: SS.
Cast off.

Making up

1 Sew up the shoulder seam.
2 Cast on 26sts with brown for waist strap, then cast off.
3 Sew one end of the strap to the bottom front corner and a press stud to the other end. Sew the receiving end of the stud on the back, five rows down from the shoulder seam.

Swimming

Athlete

Make a female figure in peach, with hair base in light brown.

Costume

Cast on 19 sts in variegated ribbon yarn.

rows 1–14: SS.
row 15: skpo, K to last 2 sts, K2tog.
row 16: P2tog, P to last 2 sts, P2tog tbl.
rows 17–22: rep rows 15 and 16 three times.
rows 23–24: SS.
rows 25–32: inc 1 st at both ends of every row.
rows 33–46: SS.
row 47: as row 15.
row 48: purl.
rows 49–52: rep rows 47 and 48 twice.
row 53: K3, cast off 7 sts, K to end turn.
row 54: P3. Put rem. 3 sts on holder.
row 55: working on 3 rem sts only, skpo, K1.
rows 56–71: work SS sts for shoulder strap. Cast off.
row 55: Return to 3 sts on holder, put on needle, skpo, K1.
rows 56–71: work SS sts for second shoulder strap. Cast off.

Making up

1 Sew up the side seams of the costume.
2 Cross the shoulder straps over at the back and stitch the ends to each side of the cast-on edge.
3 Run a thread of yarn along the cast-on edge to tighten the costume up a little if the back drops when you try it on the figure.

Swimming cap

Make one, following the instructions for the crash helmet on page 41, using variegated ribbon yarn.

You will need

Needles 3mm (US 3)
Yarns 50g ball of ribbon yarn in variegated colour
Toy stuffing
Sewing needle and thread

The front of the costume (top) and (bottom) the back, showing how the straps cross over one another.

Definitely not a fish out of water, Tammy knows exactly what she wants – and that's first place!

Discus

Athlete

Make a male figure in brown with white underpants, with hair base in black fun fur.

Shoes

Make two, following the instructions for trainers on page 12. Use black for the uppers, soles and laces.

Shorts

Make two. Cast on 26 sts in purple.
rows 1–6: SS.
rows 7–8: Cast off 2 sts at beg of each row.
row 9: skpo, K to last 2 sts, K2tog.
row 10: purl.
rows 11–12: rep rows 9 and 10.
rows 13–20: SS. Cast off.

Making up

1 Sew each leg seam up.
2 Sew both pieces together.

Top

Back

Cast on 22 sts in purple.
rows 1–8: SS.
rows 9–10: change to white, SS.
rows 11–14: change to orange, SS.
rows 15–16: change to white, SS.
rows 17–18: change to purple, cast off 2 sts at beg of each row.
row 19: skpo, K to last 2 sts, K2tog.
row 20: purl.
rows 21–22: rep rows 19 and 20.
rows 23–32: SS. Cast off.

Front

Work as back to row 22.
row 23: K2, K2tog, turn, put rem sts on holder.
row 24: purl.
row 25: K1, K2tog.
rows 26–32: SS.
Cast off. Leave the centre 6 sts on holder and return the remaining 4 sts to needle.
row 23: skpo, K2.
row 24: purl.
row 25: skpo, K1.
rows 26–32: SS. Cast off.

Sleeves

Cast on 20 sts in purple.
rows 1–8: SS.
rows 9–10: Cast off 2 sts at beg of each row.
rows 11–12: SS.
row 13: skpo, K to last 2 sts, K2tog.
row 14: purl.
rows 15–16: rep rows 13 and 14. Cast off.

Making up

1 Sew the left shoulder seam with the 2 sts from the front to the left cast-off edge of the back.
2 With purple, pick up and knit 10 sts for the back of the neck, starting 2 sts in from the right-hand edge. 8 sts down left front, 6 sts left on holder. 8 sts up right front. Cast off purlwise.
3 Sew up the right shoulder seam.
4 Sew the tops of the sleeves into the armholes.
5 Sew up the side and sleeve seams.

Discus

Cast on 10 sts in cream.
row 1: inc in every st.
rows 2–7: change to light brown, SS beg with a P row.
row 8: change to cream, purl.
row 9: K2tog to end.
Cast off purlwise.
Gather cast on sts. Fasten off.
Gather cast off sts.

Making up

Insert disc. Sew seam over the disc.

You will need

Needles 3mm (US 3)

Yarns 50g balls of DK yarn in brown, cream, white, purple, black and grey
Small amounts of DK yarn in orange and light brown
Small amount of fun fur in black
Toy stuffing
Sewing needle and thread

Backpack

Back

Cast on 14 sts in grey.
rows 1–18: SS.
row 19: skpo, K to last 2 sts, K2tog.
row 20: purl.
rows 21–28: rep rows 19 and 20 four times.
Cast off.

Side

Cast on 5 sts in grey.
rows 1–50: SS. Cast off.

Front

Cast on 14 sts in black.
rows 1–2: SS.
row 3: inc 1 st at both ends of every row.
row 4: purl.
rows 5–18: rep rows 3 and 4 seven times.
row 29: K1, (yo, K2tog) to last st, K1.
Cast off on wrong side.

Straps

Cast on 20 sts in grey.
rows 1–2: SS.
rows 3–5: knit.
rows 6–7: SS beg with a P row.
Cast off purlwise.

Making up

1 Sew the side to the front and back pieces.
2 Make two twisted cords to go through the holes at the top of the front piece and tie in

the middle. Sew one end of each cord to the inside of the backpack; one at each side where the front and side pieces meet.

3 Stitch on a press stud to close the front flap.

4 Fold the shoulder straps in half and stitch the ends up. Sew the cast-off and cast-on edges together.

5 Position the backpack on the figure to check arms can go through straps, and sew the straps to the back pack.

Kanuha Mumea has come prepared for a long day of training – he has brought a backpack to carry his discus around (and hopefully a sandwich or two).

Weightlifting

Athlete

Make a male figure in light peach with white underpants, with hair in black fun fur.

Shoes

Make two, following the instructions for trainers on page 12. Use purple for the uppers, and black for the soles and laces.

Leotard

Legs

Cast on 20 sts in purple.

rows 1–12: SS, break off yarn.

Leave sts on holder and make another leg in the same way. Do not break yarn. Transfer sts back on to a needle.

Body

row 13: K19, K2tog (a stitch from each leg), K19.

rows 14–22: SS, beg with P row.

rows 23–26: change to yellow, SS.

rows 27–28: change to purple, SS.

row 29: K8, cast off 4, K14 (15 on needle), turn, put rem sts on holder.

Front

row 30: P15.

row 31: skpo, K to last 2 sts, K2tog.

rows 32–35: rep rows 30 and 31 twice.

row 36: purl.

row 37: K2, cast off 5, K1, turn, work 13 rows on these 2 sts for shoulder straps, then cast off. With wrong side facing, rejoin yarn to the 2 sts left.

next 13 rows: SS, beg with a P row. Cast off.

Back

With right side of work facing, put 8 sts from holder on to a needle, then the 12 sts left.

next row: Rejoin yarn and cast off the first 4 sts, K to end.

next row: purl.

next row: skpo, K to last 2 sts, K2tog.

next row: purl.

next 2 rows: rep last two rows until 10 sts remain. Cast off.

Making up

1 Sew up the leg and back seams.

2 Sew a shoulder strap to the cast-off edge of the back at the beg and end of the row.

Weights

Bar

Make one. Cast on 8 sts in grey. Work SS for 18cm (7in), then thread the yarn through all the sts and pull up tight.

Large weight

Make two. Cast on 14 sts in red.

row 1: purl.

row 2: inc in every st.

rows 3–6: SS, beg with P row.

rows 7–9: knit.

rows 10–13: SS.

row 14: K2tog to end. Cast off purlwise.

Small weight

Make two. Cast on 10 sts in yellow.

row 1: purl.

row 2: inc in every st.

rows 3–5: knit.

row 6: K2tog to end. Cast off.

You will need

Needles 3mm (US 3)

Yarns 50g balls of DK yarn in light peach and purple
Small amounts of DK yarn in red, yellow and grey
Small amount of fun fur in black
Toy stuffing
Sewing needle and thread
Straight drinking straw
Two 3cm (1⅛in) plastic discs
Two 5cm (2in) plastic discs

Making up

1 Cut the straw to 18cm (7in).

2 Sew the seam of the bar for 2cm (¾in), then insert the straw and continue sewing up.

3 Gather the cast-on edge tightly and fasten it off.

4 Cut a 1cm (½in) wide hole in the centre of each of the plastic discs.

5 Sew the seam of the small weight up to the reverse ridge. Insert the 3cm (1⅛in) disc then sew up the rest of the seam.

6 Passing the needle through the hole in the middle of the disc, sew the cast-on and cast-off edges together tightly.

7 Repeat the process for the other small weight, then repeat for the large weights, using the 5cm (2in) discs.

8 Put the weights on to the bar. If you have difficulty with this, push a pencil in first to widen the hole.

Powerful Stanislav Konstantin boasts that he can lift almost anything! He has been packed full of toy stuffing so his mighty muscles bulge.

Ice Hockey

Athlete

Make a male figure in beige with white underpants, with hair base in doubled 4-ply tan yarn.

Crash helmet

Make one, following the instructions for the crash helmet on page 41, using black.

Ice skates

Make two, following the instructions on page 42, using black for the uppers, soles and laces, and white for the blades.

Shorts

Make two. Cast on 30 sts in white.
row 1: knit.
rows 2–10: change to red. SS.
rows 11–12: cast off 2 sts at beg of each row.
row 13: skpo, K to last 2 sts, K2tog.
row 14: purl.
rows 15–16: rep rows 13 and 14.
rows 17–24: SS.
Cast off.

Making up

1 Sew up the leg seams.
2 Sew up the front and back seams.

Top

Back

Cast on 28 sts in white.
row 1: knit.
rows 2–18: change to red. SS.
rows 19–20: Cast off 2 sts at beg of each row.
row 21: skpo, K to last 2 sts, K2tog.
row 22: purl.
rows 23–34: rep rows 21 and 22 six times.
Cast off.

Front

Work as back until row 30 (14 sts).
row 31: skpo, K1, K2tog, turn, put the other sts on the holder.
row 32: purl.
row 33: skpo, K1.
row 34: purl.
row 35: skpo. Fasten off. Leave the centre 4 sts on the holder. Return the last 5 to a needle.
row 31: skpo, K1, K2tog.
row 32: purl.
row 33: K1, K2tog.
row 34: purl.
row 35: K2tog, fasten off.

Sleeve

Cast on 18 sts in white.
row 1: knit.
rows 2–6: change to red, SS.
row 7: inc 1 st at each end of row.
rows 8–12: SS.
rows 13–18: rep rows 7–12.
rows 19–20: Cast off 2 sts at beg of each row.
row 21: skpo, K to last 2 sts, K2tog
row 22: purl.
rows 23–34: rep rows 21 and 22 six times.
Cast off.

Making up

1 Make the neck edge as follows: using white yarn and with the right side facing, pick up and knit 3 sts down left front, 4 sts left on front holder, 3 sts up right front, 4 sts from sleeve top, 8 sts from back, 4 sts from other sleeve top. 26 sts, cast off.
2 Sew raglan seams.
3 Sew sleeve and side seams.

You will need

Needles 3mm (US 3)

Yarns 50g balls of DK yarn in beige, red, black and white
Small amount of 4-ply yarn in tan
Toy stuffing
Sewing needle and thread
2.5cm (1in) lengths of 0.5cm (¼in) wide elastic in white

Socks

Cast on 17 sts in red.
rows 1–20: K1, P1 (rib).
Cast off.

Making up

1 Sew up the back seam.
2 When you put the socks on the legs, tuck the bottom edges inside the tops of the ice skates.

Shin pads

Make two. Cast on 12 sts in white.
rows 1–20: SS.
row 21: skpo, K to last 2 sts, K2tog.
row 22: purl.
rows 23–26: rep rows 21 and 22 twice.
rows 27–28: SS.
row 29: inc 1 st at each end of row.
row 30: purl.
rows 31–34: rep rows 29–30 twice.
rows 35–54: SS.
Cast off.

Making up

1 Sew up the side and bottom seams.
2 Sew two pieces of elastic to the back of each shin pad.

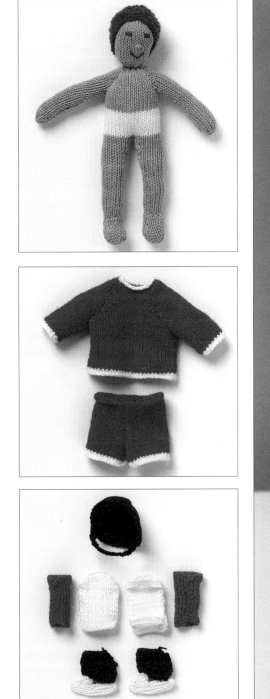

Celebrating yet another goal, Kenny Burnside skates around the edge of the rink, grandstanding for the crowd.

Snowboarding

Athlete

Make a male figure in beige with white underpants and hair base in yellow.

Shoes

Make two, following the instructions for trainers on page 12. Use black for the uppers, soles and laces.

Crash helmet

Make one, following the instructions for the crash helmet on page 41. Use white.

Trousers

Make two. Cast on 28 sts in turquoise.
rows 1–30: SS.
rows 31–32: cast off 3 sts at beg of each row.
row 33: skpo, K to last 2 sts, K2tog.
row 34: purl.
rows 35–36: rep rows 33 and 34.
rows 37–42: SS. Cast off.

Making up

1 Fold each leg piece in half and sew the leg seam up to 3 sts. Cast off.
2 Sew the two leg pieces together.

Jacket

Back

Cast on 27 sts in turquoise.
rows 1–2: SS.
rows 3–4: knit.
rows 5–8: SS.
rows 9–12: change to white. SS.
rows 13–14: change to yellow. SS.
rows 15–18: change to turquoise. SS.
rows 19–22: change to white. SS.
rows 23–24: change to yellow. SS.
rows 25–26: change to turquoise. Cast off 3 sts at beg of each row. SS.

row 27: skpo, K to last 2 sts, K2tog.
row 28: purl.
row 29: change to white. skpo, K to last 2 sts, K2tog.
row 30–32: SS, beg with P row.
row 33–34: change to yellow. SS.
rows 35–38: change to turquoise. SS. Cast off.

Left front

Cast on 15 sts in turquoise.
Work as back to row 24, continue in the same colour sequence as the back.
row 25: cast off 3 sts, P to end.
row 26: P to last 2 sts, P2tog.
row 27: knit.
rows 28–29: rep rows 26–27.
rows 30–33: SS.
row 34: Cast off 3 sts purlwise, P to end.
row 35: K to last 2 sts, K2tog.
row 36: P2tog, P to end.
rows 37–38: rep rows 35 and 36. Cast off.

Right front

Work as left front, reversing shaping.

Sleeves

Make two. Cast on 26 sts in turquoise.
rows 1–2: SS.
rows 3–5: knit.
rows 6–14: SS, beg with a P row.
row 15: skpo, K to last 2 sts, K2tog.
rows 16–22: SS, beg with a P row.
rows 23–24: cast off 3 sts at beg of each row.
row 25: skpo, K to last 2 sts, K2tog.
row 26: purl.
rows 27–28: rep rows 25–26.
Cast off.

Hood

Make one, following the instructions for the hood on page 12, using turquoise yarn.

Making up

1 Sew up the shoulder seams.

You will need

Needles 3mm (US 3)

Yarns 50g balls of DK yarn in beige, turquoise, black, white and pale blue. Small amounts of DK yarn in white, yellow, royal blue and black

Toy stuffing

Sewing needle and thread

2.5cm (1in) lengths of 0.5cm (¼in) wide elastic in black

17 x 4.5cm (6¾ x 1¾in) piece of sturdy plastic, rounded at both ends

7.5cm (3in) wide black sheer voile ribbon

Black pipe cleaner

2 Sew the hood in place.
3 Pick up and knit 16 sts evenly up the right front, then 20 sts up hood to top seam and turn.
4 Cast off 17 sts, purl to end. Knit 3 rows, purl. Cast off.
5 Work the other front to match.
6 Fold over the front facing and stitch down into the inside of the front.
7 Sew four press studs to the front facing.
8 Turn up the bottom hem and slip stitch it into place.
9 Sew up the sleeve and side seams.
10 Turn up the sleeve hems and stitch them into place.

Gloves

Make two. Cast on 16 sts in black.
rows 1–2: K1 P1 (rib).
rows 3–14: SS.
row 15: K2tog to end.
Thread yarn through sts and fasten off.

Making up

1 Sew up the side seam.
2 Repeat on the other glove.

Sweater

Make one to go under the jacket, following the instructions for the top on page 58, using pale blue yarn.

Pictured leaping into the air on a downhill run, Luke Seifert does not mind if he wins or loses as long as he can use the mountain for free-riding later.

Snowboard

Cast on 8 sts in dark blue.

rows 1–2: SS.

row 3: inc 1 st in first and last st.

row 4: purl.

rows 5–6: rep rows 3 and 4.

rows 7–46: SS until work measures 16cm (6¼in).

row 47: skpo. K to last 2 sts, K2tog.

row 48: purl.

rows 49–50: rep rows 47 and 48.

rows 51–52: SS.

row 53–102: as rows 3–52, worked in a striped pattern. Each stripe consists of six rows: two rows each in white, blue and dark blue.

Cast off.

Making up

1 Fold the work in half, sew up one side seam and insert the plastic piece.

2 Continue sewing up other side.

3 Sew the ends of one of the pieces of elastic together to make a loop, then repeat with the other piece.

4 Sew the loops to the top (plain dark blue side) of the snowboard along the central line, leaving a 2cm (¾in) gap between the two loops.

Goggles

1 Cut a piece of pipe cleaner to 17cm (6¾in) in length. Wrap black yarn all along the length of the pipe cleaner, covering it.

2 To prevent the yarn unravelling, stitch the end down using black sewing thread.

3 Bend the pipe cleaner to a right angle 5.5cm (2⅛in) in from each end, then bend it back 0.5cm (¼in) from the ends.

4 With the rest of the pipe cleaner, cut a piece big enough to bend two half circles to go over the nose for the shape of the lower part of the goggles. Bend back 1cm (½in) at the ends to go along the side bars on each side of the head. Cut this piece and wrap with black yarn.

5 With sewing thread stitch this second piece to the inside corners of the goggles at the bend and 1cm (½in) to the side bar on each side.

6 Measure the distance from the top of the goggles to the bottom. Double this and add 1cm (½in) for the seam. Cut this length of ribbon. Fold it in half. Turn under 0.5cm (¼in) at each raw edge, then oversew this edge to prevent fraying.

7 Sew the ribbon to the inside edge of the goggles all round, easing it up between the half circles of the nose area so it is not seen.

Medals

With your athletes and sports stars all knitted and ready, it is fun to have some medals for those who do well!

Medal

Make two. Cast on 1 st in either yellow, grey or light brown (for gold, silver or bronze).
row 1: inc 1 st.
row 2: inc 1 st in first st.
next rows: continue to inc 1 st in first st of every row until 8 sts. P4, turn, skpo, K2tog, P2. Cast off 2 sts.
next row: return to 4 sts remaining. With wrong side facing, P4.
next row: skpo, K2tog.
next row: P2.
Cast off.

Making up

1 Sew the two pieces together all round, leaving a small gap.
2 Stuff the yarns ends inside the heart-shaped medal, then sew up the gap.
3 Stitch a short length of ribbon to the back of the medal.

You will need

Needles 3mm (US 3)

Yarns Small amounts of DK yarn in yellow, grey and light brown

Sewing needle and thread

10cm (4in) lengths of 0.5cm (¼in) wide ribbon in colour of your choice

Make three heart-shaped medals in different colours for your own podium pose.

Publishers' Note

If you would like more books about
novelty knitting, try:

Tasty Knits by Susan Penny and
Susie Johns, Search Press 2011

Twenty to Make: Knitted Bears
by Val Pierce, Search Press 2009

*Knitted Pirates, Princesses, Witches,
Wizards and Fairies* by Annette Hefford,
Search Press 2009

If you would like more information on
knitting techniques, you might like:

Beginner's Guide to Knitting by
Alison Dupernex, Search Press 2004